WILD ABOUT

GIRAFFES

By Emma Huddleston

Kaleidoscope
Minneapolis, MN

BIGFOOT BOOKS

The Quest for Discovery Never Ends

This edition first published in 2020 by Kaleidoscope Publishing, Inc.

No part of this publication may be reproduced in whole or in part without written permission of the publisher.

For information regarding permission, write to Kaleidoscope Publishing, Inc.
6012 Blue Circle Drive
Minnetonka, MN 55343

Library of Congress Control Number
2019938836

ISBN
978-1-64519-004-2 (library bound)
978-1-64494-246-8 (paperback)
978-1-64519-104-9 (ebook)

Printed in the United States of America.

FIND ME IF YOU CAN!

Bigfoot lurks within one of the images in this book. It's up to you to find him!

TABLE OF
CONTENTS

Chapter 1: **World's Tallest Mammal** **4**

Chapter 2: **Spotted Coat** **10**

Chapter 3: **Social Life** **16**

Chapter 4: **Protecting Giraffes** **24**

Beyond the Book 28

Research Ninja 29

Further Resources 30

Glossary 31

Index 32

Photo Credits 32

About the Author 32

World's Tallest Mammal

The giraffe looks down. He can barely see his toes. Giraffes are the world's tallest **mammals**. They can be 14 to 19 feet (4.3 to 5.8 m) tall. He spends his time looking down on the world.

This giraffe's neck helps him survive. It is 6 feet (1.8 m) long. It weighs 600 pounds (272 kg). It helps him see far in the distance. He looks for **predators** and food. His neck helps him reach food at the tops of trees. Other animals can't get to it.

Giraffes are the tallest land animals.

The giraffe is at the watering hole. Other giraffes are with him. He is on guard. He watches the area for lions or crocodiles. This lets another giraffe take a risk. She is going to drink.

Watering holes are risky for giraffes. They have to get into an awkward position. She spreads her legs wide. She reaches her long neck to the ground. She drinks from the watering hole. She could be easily attacked. But giraffes watch out for each other. They are safer in groups.

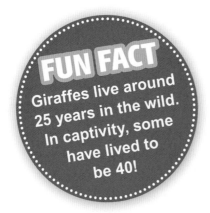

FUN FACT

Giraffes live around 25 years in the wild. In captivity, some have lived to be 40!

Drinking is difficult for giraffes because of their long legs.

Suddenly, the giraffe starts running. He spotted a lion in the distance. The other giraffes run, too. Their long legs carry them at 35 miles per hour (56 km/h) for short distances. Other animals use the giraffes as a signal. Birds fly into trees. Ground animals hide in bushes. A giraffe running is a warning that danger is coming.

Giraffes can see danger from far away.

Luckily, giraffes don't have to drink water very often. They can go several days without drinking. Most of the water they need comes from the plants they eat.

CHAPTER 2

Spotted Coat

A giraffe stops galloping. She slows down to a walk. Her legs are 6 feet (1.8 m) long. They are mostly white. Brown spots cover her body. Some spots are bigger than others. Many white lines fill the space between spots. The pattern on her **coat** is unique. No two giraffes have the same pattern.

WHAT NOISE DOES A GIRAFFE MAKE?

Many animals **communicate** with noise. Cows moo. Birds chirp. Wolves howl. People once thought giraffes were silent. But scientists discovered that they hum. This might be how they communicate.

Northern giraffes have white legs.

PARTS OF A
GIRAFFE

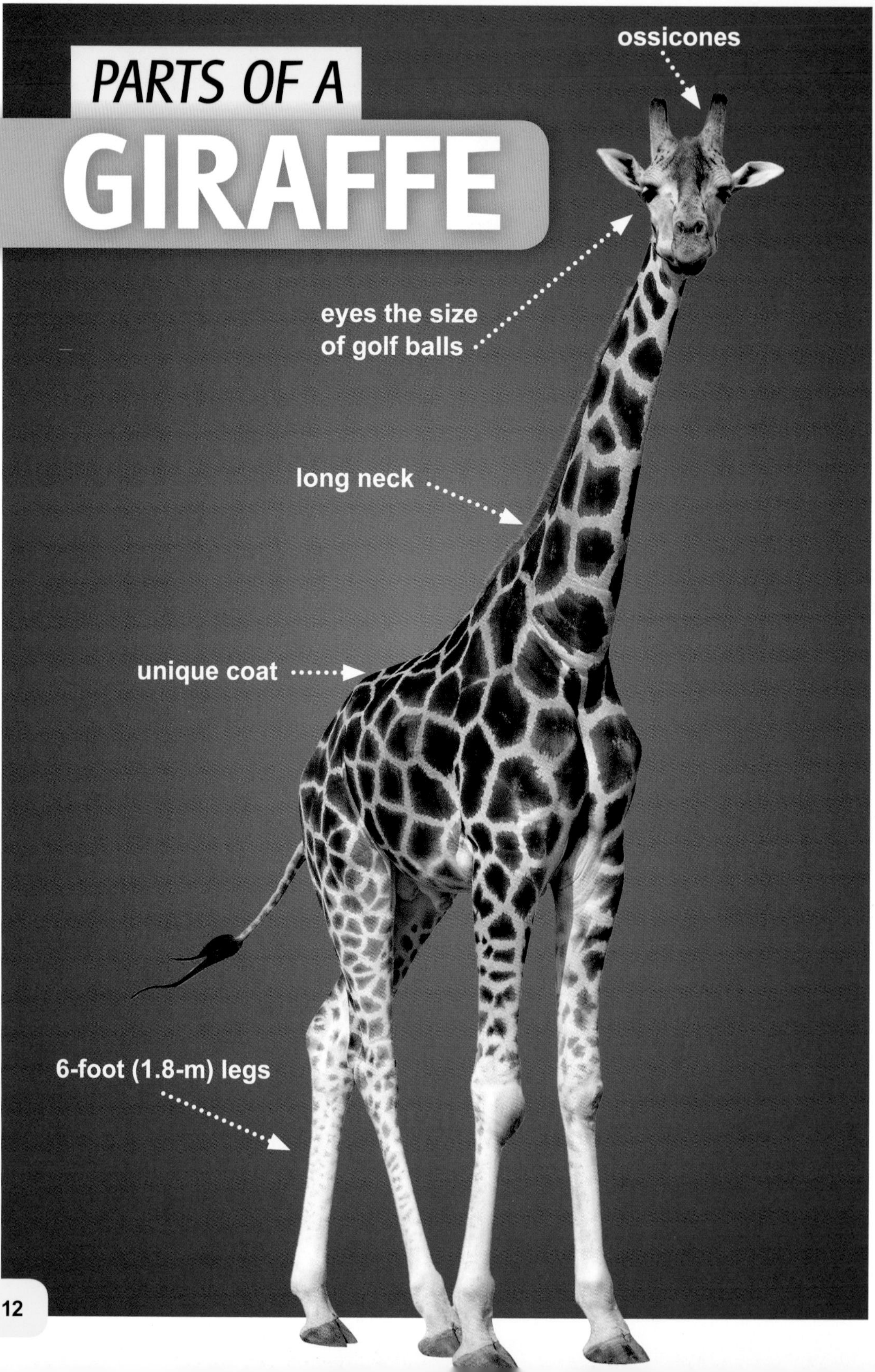

ossicones

eyes the size
of golf balls

long neck

unique coat

6-foot (1.8-m) legs

The giraffe catches her breath. Her lungs can hold 12 gallons (55 L) of air. That is more than ten times the amount human lungs can hold. Her heart beats in her chest. It weighs 25 pounds (11 kg). It is very strong. It pumps blood up her long neck to her brain.

Reticulated giraffes have big, brown-orange patches separated by white lines.

Male giraffes knock their necks together to show dominance.

Two male giraffes knock their heads together. One swings his neck and hits the other. They are necking. Necking is playful fighting. Thud! They hit again.

The larger male is 18 feet (5.5 m) tall. He weighs 3,000 pounds (1,360 kg). He is twice as heavy as the female watching. She stands 14 feet (4.2 m) tall. She weighs 1,500 pounds (680 kg). She is large for a female giraffe.

FUN FACT
Giraffes only have seven bones in their neck, like humans. But each bone is much larger.

CHAPTER 3

Social Life

A **tower** of nine giraffes walk together. Giraffes are very social. They do not attack each other for getting too close. Towers can have up to twenty members. It can be a mix of males and females. Or it can be just females and young giraffes.

Masai giraffes have jagged spots, like leaves.

The tower **roams** a savanna in Africa. Savannas are grassy plains. Some trees and bushes are scattered in the open area. Giraffes spend lots of time traveling to find food. They can eat hundreds of pounds of leaves a week. They spend sixteen to twenty hours eating every day.

The giraffes are hungry. They are **herbivores**. They look for leaves, seeds, fruit, and buds. They stick their heads into high branches. Few animals can reach the food there. Their long tongues look purple. The dark color protects the tongue from getting sunburnt.

Giraffes like to eat leaves from acacia trees. But acacia trees have thorns. One giraffe raises his head to the top of the tree. He sticks his tongue out. It is 21 inches (53 cm) long. He uses it to reach around the thorns. His spit is thick and sticky. It protects his throat from any thorns he swallows.

Giraffes use their long necks to reach leaves at the tops of trees.

FUN FACT

Giraffes' horns are called ossicones. They're made of the same stuff as human noses.

19

A female giraffe with a round belly walks slowly. She is getting ready to give birth. She stands still. A calf falls more than 5 feet (1.5 m) to the ground with a thud. He is not hurt. He takes a deep breath.

The calf stands up after thirty minutes. His skinny legs are wobbly. He takes a few steps. His legs shake. He is 6 feet (1.8 m) tall. He weighs more than 100 pounds (45 kg). He walks under his mother's legs. He drinks milk from her body. He grows 1 inch (2.54 cm) taller every day for the first week. He doesn't like to be left alone. His mother leaves to eat. He lies down. He waits for her to come back.

FUN FACT

Oxpecker birds hang out on giraffes' bodies eating fleas and ticks.

HOW BIG ARE
GIRAFFES?

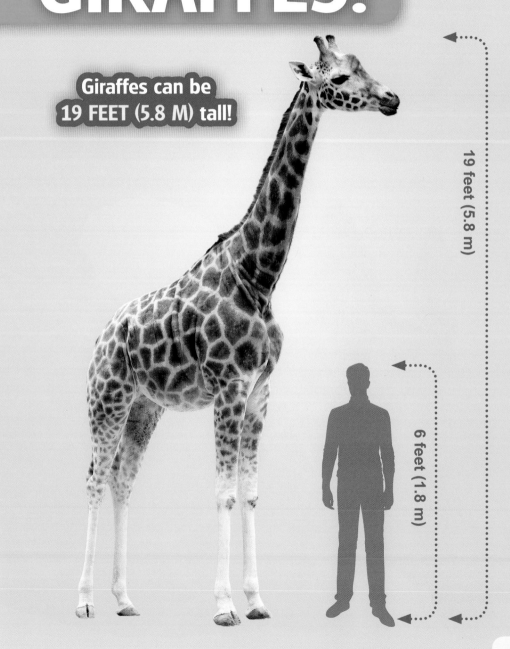

Giraffes can be
19 FEET (5.8 M) tall!

19 feet (5.8 m)

6 feet (1.8 m)

Giraffes don't sleep much. When they do, they curl up and rest their heads on their bodies.

Three young giraffes play together. They gallop across the savanna. One tries eating different leaves. The other two run in a circle around the adult. She is in charge of watching them play. The other adults are off roaming or eating. The adults help each other raise the young giraffes. Most giraffes live twenty-five years in the wild.

Another adult giraffe is napping. He sits on the ground. His legs are folded under his body. His head is curled and resting on his body. But he doesn't sleep long. He just needed a two-minute nap. Giraffes only sleep five to twenty minutes each day. Some nap standing up.

CHAPTER 4

Protecting Giraffes

David visited Africa to make a video about giraffes. They are unique animals. Their large size can make it seem like nothing can hurt them. But giraffes are **vulnerable**. Fewer than 2,000 roam central Africa. And there are fewer than 98,000 left in the wild. David's video aimed to raise awareness about giraffe **poaching**.

People hunt giraffes for different reasons. Some poor towns don't have enough food. Some want their tails. The tails are a sign of wealth. Or they can be made into fly swatters. Giraffes have no defense against guns.

David visited national parks in Africa. He met groups of people who wanted to save giraffes, too. Rangers work in parks. They watch for poachers and keep the area safe.

Poaching and loss of land have made giraffes vulnerable.

Where Do Giraffes Live?

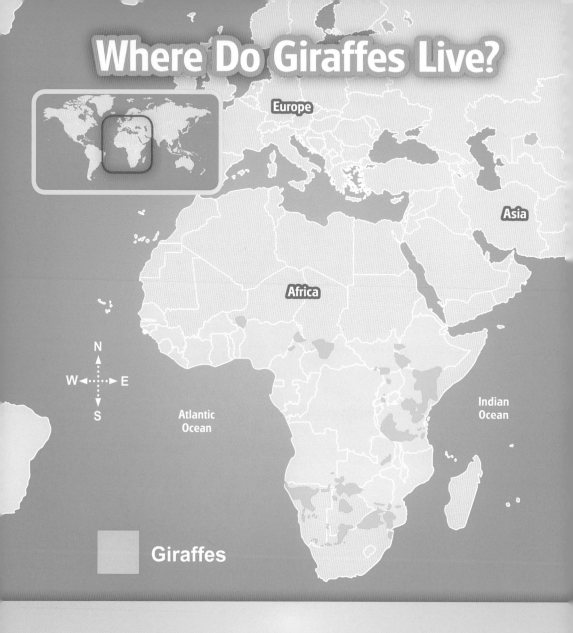

Europe

Asia

Africa

Atlantic
Ocean

Indian
Ocean

N
W ◄┈┈►E
S

Giraffes

Rebecca looked across Lake Baringo in Kenya. She visited the conservancy there in 2018. Conservancies protect wildlife. This one was helping bring giraffes back to the area. They had disappeared from this area for seventy years.

Rebecca thought about what changed in recent years. Cities throughout Africa had grown. Wildlife areas shrank. Trees were cut down for building. Farmers used more land. She knew giraffes needed lots of space and food. But places in Africa had changed. Human actions threatened giraffes.

Luckily, conservancies like this one helped giraffes. Rebecca saw that this area was a perfect **habitat** for them. It had green hills and acacia trees. There was space to roam and plenty of food. Six giraffes lived there in 2018. She hoped the group would continue to grow.

Lots of people want to help giraffes.

BEYOND
THE BOOK

After reading the book, it's time to think about what you learned.
Try the following exercises to jumpstart your ideas.

THINK

THAT'S NEWS TO ME. Many giraffes live around the world in zoos and conservancies. Consider how news sources might be able to fill in more details about giraffes in zoos and conservancies. What new information could be found in news articles? Where can you find those news sources?

CREATE

PRIMARY SOURCES. A primary source is an original document, photograph, or interview. Make a list of different primary sources you might be able to find about giraffes. What new information might you learn from these sources?

SHARE

SUM IT UP. Write one paragraph summarizing important points from this book. Make sure it's in your own words. Don't just copy what is in the text. Share the paragraph with a classmate. Does your classmate have any comments about the summary? Do they have additional questions about giraffes?

GROW

DRAWING CONNECTIONS. Create a drawing that shows and explains connections between savannas and giraffes. What things in this habitat help a giraffe survive? What dangers do giraffes face there? How does learning about savannas help you better understand giraffes?

RESEARCH NINJA

Visit *www.ninjaresearcher.com/0042* to learn how
to take your research skills and book report writing to the next level!

RESEARCH ....

DIGITAL LITERACY TOOLS

SEARCH LIKE A PRO
Learn about how to use search engines to find useful websites.

FACT OR FAKE?
Discover how you can tell a trusted website from an untrustworthy resource.

TEXT DETECTIVE
Explore how to zero in on the information you need most.

SHOW YOUR WORK
Research responsibly— learn how to cite sources.

WRITE ....

GET TO THE POINT
Learn how to express your main ideas.

PLAN OF ATTACK
Learn prewriting exercises and create an outline.

DOWNLOADABLE REPORT FORMS

Further Resources

BOOKS

Bell, Samantha. *Meet a Baby Giraffe.* Lerner Publications, 2016.

Dussling, Jennifer. *Giraffes.* Penguin Young Readers, 2016.

Murray, Julie. *Giraffes.* Abdo Publishing, 2012.

WEBSITES

Factsurfer.com gives you a safe, fun way to find more information.

1. Go to www.factsurfer.com.

2. Enter "Giraffes" into the search box and click Q.

3. Select your book cover to see a list of related websites.

Glossary

calf: A calf is a baby giraffe. A calf is already 6 feet (1.8 m) tall when it is born.

coat: A coat is the skin and fur covering a giraffe's body. No two giraffes have the same pattern on their coat.

communicate: To communicate is to send messages by talking, making noise, or moving the body. Scientists think giraffes communicate by humming.

habitat: A habitat is the place where an animal lives. Acacia trees are part of a giraffe's habitat.

herbivores: Herbivores are animals that only eat plants, not meat. Giraffes are herbivores.

mammals: Animals that are mammals give birth, drink milk from the mother, and have hair. Giraffes are mammals, and calves drink their mother's milk for up to a year.

poaching: Poaching is illegal hunting. Giraffes are in danger from poaching because hunters want their unique coats.

predators: Predators are animals that hunt and eat other animals. Giraffes use their long necks to watch for predators in the distance.

roams: When an animal roams, it travels from place to place. A giraffe roams to find more food to eat.

tower: A tower is a group of giraffes. A tower of giraffes can have up to twenty members.

vulnerable: An animal is vulnerable when it is in danger of being hurt. Giraffes are vulnerable in the wild.

Index

acacia trees, 18

breathing, 13, 20

calves, 20–23

drinking, 6, 9

eating, 5, 9, 17–20, 23

legs, 6–8, 10, 12, 20, 23

lions, 6, 8

mammals, 4, 20

necks, 5–6, 12, 13, 15, 18

noises, 10

ossicones, 12, 19

oxpecker birds, 20

poaching, 24

reserves, 24–27

savannas, 17, 23

size, 4–5, 15, 20, 21

sleeping, 23

spots, 10

tongues, 18

towers, 16–17, 23

where giraffes live, 17, 24–27

PHOTO CREDITS

ABOUT THE AUTHOR

Emma Huddleston has written books about science, sports, animals, and more. She thinks animals are fascinating. When she isn't writing, she enjoys reading and swing dancing. She lives in the Twin Cities with her husband.